2020
A Year of Fortune

365 Statements that Inspire, Motivate & Encourage

Natasha E. Williams

A Think Rich Chick Book

2020: A Year of Fortune:
365 Statements that Inspire, Motivate & Encourage

Published in 2020 by Pretty Posh Press
Copyright © 2020 by Natasha E. Williams
Cover Design by Natasha E. Williams
Image: Pixabay.com, Creative Commons License

ISBN: 978-1-7345262-0-2
ISBN: 978-1-7345262-1-9 (eBook)
ISBN: 978-1-7345262-2-6 (journal)

All rights reserved. No part of this book may be reproduced or transmitted in any form or by any means without written permission of the author.

The contents herein is intended to be used for entertainment purposes only and not intended to be used as therapy or medical advice. Please consult a licensed professional for therapeutic or medical advice.

A Note from the Author

I received the inspiration for this book at a time when I was surrounded by negativity and was looking for ways to self-motivate I couldn't find exactly what I was looking for so I decided to create it for myself...to create the words I wanted to hear on a daily basis to keep my inspired and motivated to achieve my dreams in spite of the difficulties or road blocks that I was facing.

Months later as I was putting on the finishing touches of this book I heard from my mother that one of her friend's granddaughter was found dead in her dorm room at her university. She had committed suicide by hanging. It is so sad to be gone so young for whatever reason. I do not know her personally or what she was going through at the moment for her to make that life ending decision but I wished I could have given her some words of encouragement that no matter how hard life seemed at the moment; everything could change in an instant.

Life is tough. That is granted but there are always ups and downs; however, I truly believe that there is possibility for things to turn around. I also wish she could have read this book. If she had then just maybe it would have given her the courage to press on for another day for a better future tomorrow.

So, I write this book for everyone who needs a little or a lot of encouragement, inspiration, motivation or that extra "oomph" to keep you moving forward towards your goals and a better life. No matter what you are currently going through or that life throws your way, remember the sun will rise in the morning and this will be a year of fortune for you! Believe it to receive it.

xoxo
Natasha

Introduction

A Year of Fortune is a small but impactful book of positive statements that inspire, motivate and encourage. There is one for each day of the year. In the Chinese New Year Calendar, 2020 marks the Year of the Rat which is the first of all zodiac animals. The Rat also represents the beginning of a new day.

In Chinese culture, rats were seen as a sign of wealth and surplus. Rats are clever, quick thinkers; successful, but content with living a quiet and peaceful life. Recent years of the Rat are: 1924, 1936, 1948, 1960, 1972, 1984, 1996, 2008, and 2020.

In Christianity 2020 also marks the year of new beginnings and new starts. It is the year of divine acceleration and impact. This means good fortune is coming to you fast and powerful throughout the year. It will be the year your life changes for the better. Believe it to receive it!

This book will help you to:
- Get inspired.
- Get motivated.
- Get encouraged.
- Get the courage to start living the life of your dreams.

If you have been waiting for the perfect opportunity to make a change, start something new or make a move toward your dreams then this is the year to do it because favor and luck is on your side.

How to Use this Book

1 Read the fortune or quote for the day.

2 Think about how it relates to your life or situation.

3 Believe it to receive it. Good fortune flows where attention goes.

4 Feel what feelings come to the surface.

5 In your "Year of Fortune" journal write down thoughts, reflections, inspiration, or affirmations.

6 Refer to the fortune and your reflections throughout the day. Envision it coming into your life and feel how you will feel when it does.

1 A year of fortune awaits you. Don't be afraid to Dream Big!

2 This is your year of future. Set goals and plans and watch them materialize.

3 Good things happen when you plan ahead.

4 Preparation meets opportunity. Be prepared to take action when opportunity presents itself.

5 Promotions, bonuses and financial rewards are all possible at this time.

6 Think good thoughts and good fortune will be drawn to you.

7 This is a leap year. Take a leap yourself toward the direction of your dreams.

8 Focus on the positives instead of the negatives.

9
A positive force will enter your life to change it for the better.

10
Opportunities you have been wishing for suddenly arrive this year.

11 You can have anything you want—anything your heart desires. You can turn your ideas into Money if you simply Believe.

12 Use positive affirmations to raise your frequency to create your abundance. For example, a wonderful affirmation is simply: "I have an abundance of money" or "I always have more than enough money for everything I need".

13 Think positive! Thinking positively creates favorable situations in your life.

14 Expect to have good fortune because whatever the mind expects, it finds.

15 Anticipate happiness, joy, health and successful results for each situation and action.

16 Decide that this year you're going to go for it. Nothing is going to happen or change in your life or in your business until you decide. It's all up to you.

17
*N*ow is the time to take another look at a dream long given up on.

18
*R*emember there is no try, only do!

19
Energy flows where attention goes so focus your attention on wealth and increase.

20
Ask the Universe for what you want, and then stay open to answers in the form of clues, signs, coincidences, synchronistic events and messages.

21

Now is the time to take control over your finances and focus on being debt free. Get better rates on debt, lines of credit and credit cards.

Contact lenders today.

22

There is a connection between success and having faith. Be sure to make the connection.

23
A positive outcome to a problem is on the way.

24
The way to good fortune is paved with Yeses! Don't be afraid to ask then follow the Yeses!

25
Now is the time to allow your intuition to guide you.

26
This year is the year to be wise. Be aware of what or who is influencing you and your decisions.

27 You have access to divine guidance through your heart center. Take a few minutes each day to hear from within.

28 Don't disregard your inner urgings that your intuition flows from and take the time to listen to your heart.

29

Challenges are growth for the soul. Accept challenges with courage and don't take each challenge personally.

30

Show gratitude for the things you do have.

31 Embrace change; don't fight against it for change is inevitable.

32 Make time for your own personal happiness. Do what you love first.

33
Don't put off for tomorrow what you can get accomplished today.

34
Welcome abundance into your life.

35
The fruits of your hard work continue to grow and will pay off soon.

36
The fruits of your hard work continue to grow and will pay off soon.

37
This year spend more time resting and recharging your batteries so that you can be prepared for all the greatness coming your way in the year to come.

38
Don't be afraid to shine.

39 Move beyond pettiness and petty people.

40 Believe in the power of visualization. It works.

41
Practice wealth affirmations daily to draw more wealth to you.

42
You have the right to be rich.

43 Wealth is waiting for you to claim it.

44 Each day set mini-goals that will bring you closer to your ultimate desires.

45
Don't be afraid to say, No when you really need to.

46
Reframe from evaluating life and situations from an ego point of view but more from a soul point of view.

47

Money flows where there is a purpose for it to flow.

48

Now is the time for you to rise and start living on purpose again.

49 *Trust the process.*

50 *Abundance awaits you. Pay attention to the guidance you receive.*

51 Always be the best version of You!

52 Dream Boldly. Think Big. Aim High!

53 You will achieve your greatest success in the next year if you stay focused on the goal.

54 Now is the time to do what feels right.

55

You are bigger than any problems you face.

56

Live with an attitude of expectancy. Always expect something wonderful to happen.

57
Remember to have fun on your way to success.

58
Give cheerfully and accept gratefully.

59 It is better to pray for guidance than to drown in sorrow.

60 Don't sweat the small stuff and most of it is really small stuff.

61 *The best is yet to come!*

62 *The life you want is waiting for you. Go get it!*

63

Don't worry, just sparkle!

64

Find satisfaction in the little things you experience every day.

65
A new day always brings with it a chance for a new beginning.

66
Start creating new ideas. The minute you concentrate on your idea, new thoughts, new ideas, new measures, new ways and new methods are opened up to help make it a reality.

67

If things this year seem unfair, you could focus on the negatives, or you could focus on the future and realize that this time is meant to set up opportunities for the long term and practice the elements that will make you successful in your future endeavors.

68

Ditch your comfort zone.

69 On the other side of fear is Everything you have ever wanted.

70 A thought is mighty but a thought of love is the most powerful force in the universe.

71 Your world and your reality is created through your thoughts.

72 Life is like a block of clay and you are the artist. Fashion the clay into the life you desire.

73 Be open to change because change is inevitable.

74 What you send out into the world returns to you like a boomerang.

75 Your life is waiting for you to release it to its greatest good.

76 Money is all yours. It wants you and you want it. All you have to do is Claim It.

77
Do not run away from problems because wherever you go, there you are.

78
Re-examine any limiting beliefs that may be holding back abundance in your life.

79

The longest journey started with a single step. Do not be afraid to take that first step.

80

You have more to give to the world than you realize.

81

Keep it simple. Simple is better in all things. Complexity only adds unnecessary steps.

82

Today is the day that everything in your life changes for the better.

83 It's time to be fearless. You can have whatever you want if you decide to take action and go for it and don't let fear stop it.

84 Do only thing keeping you from your dreams is yourself.

85
Do not settle for less than the best. Do not accept anything but first place.

86
It's time to re-evaluate a situation because you are currently missing an opportunity.

87
When things do not turn out the way you'd hope, remember that there is something better coming along.

88
Have faith that everything happens for a reason.

89

An influx of abundance is headed your way this year in the form of a pay increase, promotion, or unexpected money.

90

It is important to be adaptable. You will be successful faster if you are.

91 Recognition for high quality work is coming.

92 It's a good time to join a club, organization or a group where you will meet valuable contacts for future endeavors.

93

Beware of being too frivolous or too cautious with money. A balanced approached is best.

94

Stay alert to new possibilities and new opportunities.

95 Be willing to accept help from others. You don't have to do it alone.

96 The answer to a long awaited question is on the horizon.

97

It's important that you care for your physical health, emotional health as well as your financial health.

98

It is the perfect time to start increasing your retirement savings.

99 It's time to learn something new for a future opportunity that will present itself.

100 Your dedication, skill and talents are appreciated and will soon be rewarded.

101

If you have considered venturing into a small business opportunity, this is the year to look more deeply into it.

102

Your self-reliance, wisdom and restraint will soon pay off.

103 Abundance and financial security is at hand.

104 More creative ideas will present themselves and allow you the opportunity to make money from them if you act on them.

105

You will meet new friends who will expose you to new things.

106

Family life will be happy, strong, secure and peaceful.

107

You will receive good news regarding financial matters.

108

Your plans move successfully forward at a steady pace.

109

A new interest, hobby or passion will change your life for the better.

110

You will receive good advice from a well-respected person.

111

A loyal, dedicated and dependable person will enter your life.

112

Something you have wanted to do or experience for a long time will finally be fulfilled.

113

Deal with challenges in a kind and understanding manner.

114

Remember to enjoy time with family and friends you have been neglecting.

115 Beautiful things are coming your way.

116 You will reconnect with a friend from the past.

117

A successful period in life is fast approaching.

118

Current projects will go well.

119

That which you have long awaited suddenly arrives.

120

You have been blessed with the Midas Touch! Procrastinate no longer.

121

The end of a difficult situation is on the horizon.

122

A step is required at the beginning of every journey taken. Start taking the much needed steps you have been avoiding for far too long.

123

The Universe is dreaming a bigger dream for you than you could ever dream for yourself.

124

Recovering from an ailment is on the way.

125 You draw great comfort from those around you.

126 When the fight or flight urges kick in, remember to stand your ground and fight.

127

Don't put off tomorrow what you can get done today.

128

Your circumstances will improve.

129

From this experience only good will come from it. All is well and you are safe.

130

Unconditionally allow things to be the way they are.

131
Always tell the truth and communicate fully.

132
Engage life with enthusiasm exactly as it is regardless of your likes and dislikes or your preferences, ideas, beliefs and opinions about how you think things should be or could be. In this moment, just live.

133

Your current projects will go well.

134

An unlimited supply of ideas are available to you. Claim them.

135

Your talents and skills will bring you great rewards.

136

You are about to take a quantum leap that will carry you to higher level of performance without a time consuming struggle.

137

Wealth is there for you but you need to figure out two things: Where you are and where you are going.

138

Today see what today brings for you can only see with the naked eye what will be as of now for tomorrow is a new day with new possibilities and experiences as well as challenges.

139

You will be offered new opportunities. Accept them and have confidence that you will succeed.

140

Live life on purpose.

141

If you haven't already, ask for what you want for how can you receive it if you haven't asked for it?

142

When the shape of your body no longer matches the shape of your beliefs, unwanted weight disappears.

143

Change your thoughts from lack of money to more than enough.

144

Listen to your intuition. It has the answers to all your questions, solutions to your problems and will tell you everything you need to know. You just need to get still and listen.

145

A foundation built right can carry the weight of anything it was designed to hold.

146

It's a good time to bet on your skills and talents in new and different arenas. Don't be afraid to stretch or go outside your comfort zone.

147

Dream Big! If your dreams don't scare you then they are not big enough.

148

A sea of opportunities will wash over you and wake you up to your true potential.

149

You can expect miracles when your higher consciousness is aligned with your prosperity consciousness.

150

Your community will bring you joy. If it does not, it's time to find a new community that is happier and likeminded.

151

Now is time to assess your willingness to be authentic and real. Stand tall, hold your head high and be you.

152

A prosperous life awaits you. Now is the time to make calculated actions. When you fail to plan, you plan to fail.

153

Unnecessary weight will be lifted. It is time to let go of other people's problems and other people's drama.

154

You are getting closer to the happiness you seek.

155

Beware to not allow yourself to be overburdened and overwhelmed.

156

All your hard work and efforts are starting to pay off in ways you may not have anticipated.

157

They say that good things come to those who wait. Well, the wait is over. Good things are coming.

158

Seeds planted in the past start to bloom today.

159

The fear of failure paralyzes behavior, clouds thinking and causes inaction and a person to feel stuck. You are getting unstuck this year.

160

Today's decisions are tomorrow's reality.

161

Nothing is out of reach. There is no such thing as being too ambitious! It's time to raise the bar on your expectations.

162

There is somebody waiting and needing what you have to offer.

163

Successful people are the mirror of the thoughts you rejected for yourself. Raise your self-confidence. You need it to claim your success.

164

Your aspirations for success and prosperity assume form in the year to come.

165

Your heart will soften and be made anew if you have experience betrayal in your past. Betrayal is a sign that it is time to prune away those who do not deserve your trust and have no place in your life.

166

The Universe has awesome plans for you. Make space for them in your life.

167

Someone will enter your life this year who will be instrumental in your journey.

168

Your passion turns into a profit making venture in the coming year.

169

Your hunches will pay large dividends if you pay attention and take action.

170

Magic begins to happen. Trust your heart to lead and guide you.

171

The genius of the collective consciousness is available to you. It is a place where all that was, is or will be resides. Tap into it.

172

Relief from stress and anxiety is coming. Listen to your heart and soul and express your true self.

173

Endings albeit sad are a sign of new beginnings. Something old has to go to make room for something new.

174

New doors open where old ones appear to have been previously closed.

175

Be on the look-out to be presented with a promising business opportunity or contract.

176

Stay open to creative ideas or new perspectives.

177

Take it easy this year and don't take things so seriously. Lighten up and take a more playful approach to handling difficult situations.

178

Trust the way the light is shining as you enter your most prosperous season yet.

179

You will soon have time to enjoy some small luxuries in life for a job well-done.

180

Get ready for celebration. You will certainly have something to celebrate soon.

181

There is no shortage of opportunities, just a perceived shortage of creativity and imagination.

182

Life is a cycle. You are either in a problem, heading towards a problem or coming out of a problem. This year, you are coming out and moving forward.

183

You are only in control of your own life. So let go or be dragged.

184

Be new, think new and open your heart to new things.

185

Success is finally taking shape and is yours for the claiming.

186

Breath is life so don't forget to breathe.

187

Let go of things, people and situations that bring unnecessary stress into your life.

188

New passions awaken.

189

A new love affair or renewed love flourishes.

190

Lost money is now found.

191

Your most heartfelt desires are coming true.

192

A new business venture comes your way.

193

New friends join your circle.

194

Whatever you may have perceived as a failure or a loss is now being replaced with

195

You will have renewed energy and motivation to get things done.

196

It's your chance to shine. You will be thrown in the spotlight.

197

Broken friendships are mended this year.

198

A joyful family gathering awaits you.

199

You will be reacquainted with an old friend.

200

Interesting news that will change your perspective is on the way.

201

If there is no enemy within, the enemy outside can do no harm.

202

Create a vision of the world you want to see.

203

Strength, power and healing is available all the time.

204

You will be pushed in a new, positive direction.

205

Follow your Spirit and do the things that you love, and your life's purpose will be fulfilled.

206

Fight for what you want now or fight against what you don't want later. It's your choice.

207

Opportunities are all around you. Open your eyes to the possibilities.

208

Abundance is on the way. Be prepared because preparation meets opportunity.

209

The Universe loves a grateful heart and rewards gratitude with more abundance so be grateful. Start keeping a gratitude journal.

210

Willing and wanting to do something is not enough.

You must do!

211 You will have better focus and concentration this year.

212 As soon as you change your thoughts your world will change with them.

213

When your mind becomes sold on success it will refuse to accept the possibility of failure.

214

Doubt will dissipate. Doubt kills more dreams than failure ever could. It hides in the mind and takes on many disguises.

215

You are stronger than you think.

216

By facing life's challenges you will emerge stronger.

217

Look back to learn but look forward to succeed.

218

Secret to be forever young: Don't worry, Let things go and laugh often.

219

You will be respected for what you do.

220

Opened doors to bigger opportunities will propel you to greater heights.

221
Everything will realign itself in the year to come.

222
Your sense of discernment will be enhanced so that you will make better decisions.

223

Abundance surrounds you. It's time to open up to the abundance that surrounds you.

224

Your body is talking to you, listen to it.

225

Compassion is on its way. As you find compassion for others, you will find that it comes more easily for yourself.

226

Forgiveness is on the way. Forgiveness is the key to true healing.

227

You are getting a second chance at the life you desire.

228

A beautiful and smart person will enter your life.

229

All will go well with your new endeavor or project.

230

You will take an exciting adventure to a place you have never been.

231
A stranger will offer you valuable advice.

232
A well laid out plan takes life.

233
What started off as a slow crawl will gain momentum.

234
You will get something you have wanted for a long time.

235

Old pains and hurts dissolve this year.

236

You will be invited on a lovely outing and have the best time of your life.

237

Your work situation improves tremendously.

238

Others will show you great gratitude.

239

An old friend will ask for reconciliation. It's up to you to decide if you have put the past behind you.

240

You will find new money through a new stream of income.

241

A stranger will be kind to you and inspire you in some way.

242

Your priorities will get in order this year and goals will be completed.

243 You will be presented with the opportunity of a lifetime. Don't let fear be a block.

244 This year you will feel a paradigm shift.

245
A new skill will become beneficial to your future growth.

246
You will inspire someone this week.

247

Your fortitude will be stronger.

248

You will be given much needed good news.

249 Wishes get fulfilled and dreams come true in the year ahead.

250 New career opportunities present themselves. Remember to look beyond the obvious.

251
Much needed knowledge will be passed on to you that takes you to the next level.

252
Do today what you would have done tomorrow.

253

*N*o matter how life has been in the past, today is a new day with new possibilities.

254

*A*ll that you have ever wanted is about to materialize in your life this year.

255
Surround yourself with good people and you will succeed.

256
If you can dream it, you can do it!

257

Don't be afraid to try something because you think you will fail. You will be pleasantly surprised.

258

Stop doubting your greatness.

259

Like attracts like. What you release into the Universe will be attracted back to you.

260

Pay attention to the Universal Laws for they will guide you to success.

261
Cycles repeat! That which was, will certainly be again.

262
It's time to roll up your sleeves and put the work in.

263
Your hustle is worth the work.

264
Stop procrastinating and get to doing the things you want to do.

265

Every large accomplishment started with small steps.

266

Lean in to your greatness and stop doubting yourself.

267 There is no competition. There is enough for everyone to live the life of their dreams.

268 Ask, Believe, Receive!

269 Golden opportunities await you.

270 Positive thoughts will get you a lot further than negative ones.

271
Believe in your right to prosper.

272
Money flows where attention goes.

273

Birds of a feather flock together, so pay attention to who is in your flock. Someone has to go.

274

Unleash your creativity. Creative ideas will bring forth rewards.

275 Don't be afraid to take chances.

276 The yellow brick road of success is before you. Follow the path.

277
A year of wonderment is ahead.

278
Believe in your dreams and they will start to come true.

279
What you want is already waiting for you to claim it.

280
Be enthusiastic about life. It's about to get really good.

281

This is the year things start to fall into place.

282

Don't sweat the small stuff and most of it is all "small stuff".

283 Happiness awaits you. Claim it!

284 The dreams of your heart are there for a reason. Believe they can come true.

285

You have to have patience on your journey to greatness.

286

Everything happens for a reason. Know the reason and learn the lesson.

287
The desires of your heart will manifest.

288
Showing compassion for others lead to great happiness.

289
Don't be afraid to pay good deeds forward because all will come back to you.

290
Be generous and watch abundance return ten fold.

291

Having a kind heart nurtures the soul.

292

Great things come when you least expect it.

293

Show someone love today and love returns to you.

294

Whatever you ask for you will receive.

295

A selfless nature brings tons of rewards.

296

*L*ook beyond circumstances to see what is possible in the future.

297

*Live a little;
Love a lot.*

298

Life isn't perfect but gratitude, perseverance and determination overcomes all.

299

If things don't turn out the way you want, know that there is always something better around the corner.

300

It's time to decide whether to switch, pivot or quit to get the results you seek.

301
Old hurts fade away this year to make room for joyous experiences.

302
New experiences await you.

303 More adventure is coming your way.

304 Don't be afraid to take an important step. Action takers are money makers.

305
A renewed love awakens for a project or relationship.

306
Passion knocks. Be sure to listen.

307

Miracles happen daily, so expect a miracle every day.

308

Go on an adventure to tap into untapped talents.

309

This is the year great things begin to happen in your life.

310

This is the year where you make astounding progress.

311

You will get clarity on a situation that has been bothering you.

312

The world is full of "Yeses"! Don't be afraid to ask for help.

313

Ideas will be abundance in the year to come.

314

It's time to be courageous. Don't allow fear to stop you.

315
Let your actions be an example to others.

316
It will be very important in the year ahead for you to do what you say and say what you do.

317

It's time to do what you love and love what you do.

318

Take it one day at a time. Be careful not to get ahead of yourself.

319

Change is inevitable but all change is not bad.

320

Go with the flow of things.

321
Thinking rich will draw riches to you.

322
Doors of opportunities open.

323
It's okay to start small but remember to think big!

324
Others will be inspired by what you do.

325

Quit playing small for you will do great things in the world.

326

Greatness is upon you.

327
If your dream is larger than your personal development, it will get stuck.

328
Your life is about to be elevated to the next level.

329 Create your own vision for success.

330 Many new opportunities appear in your life. Be open to receive them.

331

Quit thinking small and start thinking Big.

332

Each morning make declarations about your life.

333

Listen to your gut instincts. All money is not good money.

334

You are a Bad Ass so start acting like it.

335
Your passion turns into profit in the coming year.

336
There is nothing you can't do if you put your mind to it.

337
You don't have to wait until you get credentials or notoriety before you start.

338
Never give up hope.

339

Go for it...then keep going!

340

Next level thinking will propel you to where you want to go.

341

Be fearless!
What would you
do if you weren't
afraid?

342

Always assume
the door is open.

343
Difficult roads lead to beautiful destinations.

344
Your aspirations are your possibilities.

345

The more consistent you are the more consistent your money will be. – Boss Babe Society

346

It is time to overcome under dreaming.

347 Financial independence is yours. Claim it!

348 Inherent in every desire is the mechanics for its fulfillment. - Deepak Choprah

349
Abundance flows where energy goes.

350
A stranger will give you valuable advice.

351
If you don't work towards your dreams you will be working towards someone else's.

352
Creating 5 Goals a day keeps the Universe at play.

353

Great things never come from the comfort zone.

354

Show gratitude and more of the things you are grateful for will materialize in your life.

355

Imagine what you want until it manifests.

356

If your dreams don't scare you then they are too small.

357

You are a magnet for opportunities.

358

Believe in something greater than yourself.

359 Those who don't believe in magic will never find it. - Roald Dahl

360 Nurture your mind with great thoughts, then write them down.

361

All that glitters isn't gold. Remember to see beyond the superficial.

362

This is the year all your dreams start coming true.

363
You will experience a sense of completion this year.

364
Believe in the totality of possibilities.

365

Believe in Miracles!
Bonus

Secret to manifesting your heart's desires is to write it down. There is something powerful between the brain and writing. When you write down what you want it jump starts the law of attraction in order for it to manifest into the world. Write it down, watch it happen.

About the Author

NATASHA WILLIAMS is a natural intuitive and an avid believer in the law of attraction and the power of using visualization, thoughts, positive words, affirmations and imagination to change your life.

She has written inspirational material for nearly three decades and was on the development team for two, Chicken Soup for the Soul®, books. She has also sold her creative projects to Hollywood producers.

She lives in California with her family and when she is not writing or traveling she is creating something new.

Speaking engagements and consulting:
info@PrettyPoshPress.com
Insta: @ThinkRichChick

www.ingramcontent.com/pod-product-compliance
Lightning Source LLC
LaVergne TN
LVHW051556070426
835507LV00021B/2612